Dealing With Diversity

Media Course Study Guide

Fourth Edition

J. Q. Adams, Ph. D.

Professor of Educational and Interdisciplinary Studies

Department of Educational and Interdisciplinary Studies

Western Illinois University

Macomb, Illinois 61455

Produced by:

Governors State University

University Park, IL 60466

KENDALL/HUNT PUBLISHING COMPANY
4050 Westmark Drive   Dubuque, Iowa 52002

Copyright © 1995, 1997, 2001, 2008 by Governors State University

ISBN 978-0-7575-4772-0

Printed in the United States of America
10 9 8 7 6 5 4 3 2 1

Dealing with Diversity
TABLE OF CONTENTS

Acknowledgements

The producers wish sincerely to thank the following individuals for their contribution to the course:

Media Course Students

Nadia Abusumayah

Lina Acosta

Jacqueline Crims

Shana Dobie

Laura Dominski

Eugene Dumas

Juanita Dumas

Dartina Dunlap

Gwendolyn Grant

Carl Griggs

Josephine Guzman

Bernadette Lillard

LaThica Long

Maisha Lowery

Barbara Melton

Janet Morris

Edward OKennard

Raul Ortiz

Fernando Rayas

Kathryn Skerrett

Homer Talbert III

Monique Tarleton

Sharon Taylor

Andrew Wheeler

INTRODUCTION

Course Description

Living in the U.S.A. in the 21st century poses some of the most complex challenges this nation has ever faced. The 4th Wave (post-industrial age) has created changes in almost every facet of American life. Our dependence on technology and fossil fuels, our addiction to 24/7 media, the changes in immigration, and the unparalleled quest to accumulate personal property have all created increased class stratification as well as segregation throughout our society. The nuclear family has morphed to include more single-parent or blended families than ever, and the traditional structure of mother and father has been challenged by new adult combinations and new ways of procreating and raising children. The results of 9/11 have changed the way we protect our borders and travel. The war on terrorism has created tensions which require a greater understanding of the Judeo-Christian-Muslim history and traditions. Global interdependence has brought the world closer together which means the impact of natural disasters, hunger, disease, and international conflicts now affects the whole planet.

This course was developed to help you recognize and appreciate the differences and the similarities among diverse groups and individuals in a multicultural society. It is our hope that with this knowledge you will be able to make a difference in your spheres of influence. We challenge you to become a facilitator for improving intra/inter-cultural relations at work, in your community, and in the global village.

Expected Student Outcomes

At the end of the course you should be able to:

1. Recognize the societal implications of our nation's changing demographics.
2. Explain the importance of understanding and respecting cultural differences.
3. Develop strategies to promote intercultural awareness between different groups and among individuals within these groups.

Required Readings
Adams, J. Q. and Strother-Adams, Pearlie. (2008). *Dealing With Diversity: The Anthology 2nd Edition.* Dubuque, IA. Kendall/Hunt Publishing Company.

Course Structure

The media recordings are of live in-studio interactive classroom. The participants are students who are taking the course for credit a Governors State University, who are sometimes joined by in studio guests with knowledge in specific areas of study. Many programs also contain inserts of interviews made with guests on location or of mini-case studies. This is the third edition of my Dealing with Diversity media course, and some of the segments from the first two editions are shown again in this new edition.

How to Use This Study Guide

The student study guide is designed to assist you throughout this course. Each program is summarized with key concepts, reading assignments, and discussion questions. With each video-insert, I have supplied questions for you to answer. Read the questions before you watch each program. Once you have completed the whole program, answer the discussion questions. Suggestions for additional readings and resources are also included at the end of each class. Be sure to follow the order set out in the study guide in order to maximize your understanding of course content.

I hope you will find taking this course a very enjoyable and rewarding experience.

J. Q. Adams, Ph.D.
Professor of Education
Department of Educational and Interdisciplinary Studies
Western Illinois University
Macomb, Illinois 61455

COURSE CONTENT

Program 1
Introduction and Overview: Who in the World Is in Here?
Explore your peers' and your own individual ethnic/racial, religious, and cultural backgrounds.

Program 2
Social Interaction in Diverse Settings: The SIM's Model
Discuss how to use the Social Interaction Model (SIM) as an analytical tool for understanding human behavior in social settings.

Program 3
Negotiating Cultural Communication
Explore some of the varieties of communication styles in the U.S. as well as in other cultures around the world. Studio Guests: Isabel Lamptey, Western Illinois University, and Michel Nguessan, Governors State University. Video Insert: Asma Abdullah and Peter Shepherd, an Islamic couple from Malaysia.

Program 4
The Changing Face of America and the World
Profile the rapidly changing demographic trends affecting the U.S. and other countries around the world. Studio Guest: Michel Nguessan. Video Inserts: Plaza De Los Angeles; Professor Alexander Astin, UCLA; and Wave Theory.

Program 5
Immigration and the New Immigrants
Learn the history of Immigration laws and social policies in the U.S. Studio Guest: Fred Tsao, Policy Director at the Illinois Coalition for Immigrant and Refugee Rights. Video Inserts: Marian Smith of the Immigration and Naturalization Service (INS); White Racialist David Duke; and Marcelo Suarez, former director of Harvard University's Immigration Study.

Program 6
Race: The World's Most Dangerous Myth
Explore one of our nation's most complex and difficult problems, the concept of race. Video Insert: Dr. Michael Omi, Professor of Ethnic Studies at the University of California at Berkeley.

Program 7
Social Class Issues
The impact of social economics on the lives of families and individuals in the U.S. Studio Guests: Linzey Jones, Mayor of Olympia Fields, and Don DeGraff, Mayor of South Holland, Illinois. Video Insert: White Flight in South Suburbia.

Program 8
Gender Issues
Examine the multifaceted issues surrounding gender in our society. Video Inserts: Professor Peggy McIntosh, Wellesley College, and Byron Hurt, Director of the film Hip Hop: Beyond Beats and Rhymes.

Program 9
Native Americans
Discuss the current state of indigenous people in the U.S. Studio Guest: Joseph (Standing Bear) Schranz, an Ojibwa from the Midwest Soaring Foundation. Video Inserts: Pow Wow of the Ho Chunk Nation; Native American as well as Euro-American educators from Northern Arizona University; and Little Singer Community School (LSCS), a Charter School located on a Navajo Reservation in Arizona.

Program 10
Latino Americans, Part I
A profile of some of the many groups programified under the label of Latino(na's) in the U.S. Studio Guests: Rey Flores, a columnist for Hoy Newspaper in Chicago. Video Inserts: Chuy Negrette, an ethno-historian from Chicago; Professor Carlos Munoz, Jr. at the University of California at Berkeley; Dr. Marcelo Suarez-Orozco, director of the Harvard Immigration Program; and Janet Castellanos, a Professor at the University of California at Riverside.

Program 11
Latino Americans, Part II
Studio Guests: Rey Flores, a columnist for Hoy Newspaper in Chicago and realtor/advertiser Fred Medina. Video Inserts: the Ballet Folkloric filmed during a Mexican Independence Day celebration; a mini case study of Beardstown, a small river town in central Illinois with a rapidly growing Latino population; Janet Castellanos, a Professor at the University of California at Riverside, and a film clip from the movie Crash.

Program 12
African Americans, Part I
Examines the challenges facing this unique ethnic group and how its fate continues to evolve in the U.S. Studio Guest: Jesse Jackson Jr., Congressional Representative from the 2nd District of Illinois. Video Inserts: Birmingham Civil Rights Museum in Birmingham, Alabama; a film clip from Crash; Dr. Thomas Parham a Professor from the University of California at Irvine, and Dr. V.P. Franklin a Professor at the University of California at Riverside.

Program 13
African Americans, Part II
Studio Guest: Dr. Cathy Cohen, Director of the Black Youth study and her graduate student Jamila Celestine-Michener from the University of Chicago. Video Insert: Byron Hurt, Director of the film, Hip Hop: Beyond Beats and Rhymes.

Program 14
Asian Americans
A discussion of some of the many cultures who fall under this label and live within the U.S. Studio Guests: Rui Kaneya, managing editor of the Chicago Reporter, and Tuyet Le, executive director of the Asian American Institute. Video Inserts: Dr. Michael Omi, Professor of Ethnic Studies at the University of California at Berkeley; Dr. Gargi Roysircar-Sodowsky, Director of Diversity Issues at Antioch University New England; and the Korean American community in Chicago.

Program 15
Middle Eastern and Arab-American Cultures
An introspective look at Middle-Eastern cultures in the U.S. as they appear in the media and are perceived by the American society. Studio Guest: Ahmed Rehab, Executive Director of the Council on American-Islamic Relations in Chicago.
Video Inserts: Dr. Jack Sheehan's film Reel Bad Arabs.

Program 16
Islam

The fastest growing religion in the U.S. is Islam; it is also one of the most controversial as a result of 9/11. Studio Guests: Imam Kifah Mustapha (from a Mosque located in Bridgeview, IL) who is also the Associate Director of The Mosque Foundation and
Dr. Aminah Beverly McCloud, a Professor of Islamic Studies at DePaul University.
Video Inserts: Dr. Azizan Baharuddin from the Centre for Civilizational Dialogue at the
University of Malaysia, and a mini-case study on the Islamic community in Waukegan, Illinois.

Program 17
European Americans

This program features a segment on the Amish community in Indiana and a profile of Italians in America, looking at their struggles in the past and their dreams for the future.
Studio Guests: historian and film maker Dominic Candeloro. Video Inserts: Mini-Case Study on the Amish in the U.S.; and film clips from the movie And They Came to Chicago: The Italian American Legacy.

Program 18
Creole and Mixed Ethnic Americans

A view of Americans with mixed ethnic/racial heritage. Studio Guests: Robin Tillmon, President of the Bi-racial Family Network (BFN) in the Chicago area and the child of an inter-racial marriage and Eric Glenn, the product of mixed-race parents. Video Inserts: Creole culture in New Orleans; and an "inter-racial" couple, Diane and Reggie Alsbrook, who live off the grid in New Mexico.

Program 19
Ethnocentric Groups in the USA

Examines ethnocentric views which fuel a great deal of decision-making in this in regards to where people live, work, and worship. Video Inserts: Southern Poverty Law Center (SPLC) and a segment from the documentary film, Hate.Com: Extremists on the Internet; David Duke, a White racialist with international connections; and Liebe Geft, a leader at the Simon Wiesenthal Museum of Tolerance.

Program 20
Sexual Orientation Issues

Explore the world of Gays, Lesbians, Bi-sexuals, and the Transgendered. Studio Guests:
Sylvia and Gysbert Menninga, parents of a gay child; Tamara McClatchey, a lesbian professional; and Dr. Alan Sanders, a researcher from the University of Chicago.
Video Insert: None.

Program 21
Physical/Mental Ability Issues

People with disabilities are one of the largest special interest groups in our society and yet one with the lowest visibility. Studio Guests: Robin Sweeney, Disabilities Coordinator for Governors State University and one of her advisees, Marion Kaes, a student at GSU. Video Inserts: Hiram Zayas; and Lenda Hunt.

Program 22
Age Issues: From Young to Old
Examine age issues from young to old and their social consequences. Studio Guests: Sally Furhmann, Director of the Rich Township Senior Center, Pat Klein, Youth Director for Richton Park's Youth and Family Center; and Kenneth Kramer, President of the Park Forest Chapter of AARP. Video Inserts: Age Old Stereotypes; Adult Day Care Center.

Program 23
The State of New South Africa
The Republic of South Africa is one of the world's newest democracies; it provides a unique mirror image of the U.S. at various in times in its history.
Studio Guests: Machiel van Niekerk, Consul from the South African Consulate-General in Chicago
Video Inserts: Wilmont James of the Institute for Democracy in South Africa (IDASA) and Charles Villa-Vicencio who worked for the Truth in Reconciliation Committee (TRC); Coloreds in South Africa; and students at the Cecil B. Rhodes High School.

Program 24
Diversity Issues and Answers
A review of many of the essential topics we have explored. Studio Guest: Dr. Robert D. Martin, Curator of Anthropology at the Field Museum in Chicago. Video Inserts: Jehovah's Witnesses headquarters in New York; and Maurice Ashley, the first African American International Grand Chess Master in the world.

Dealing With Diversity — Program 1
Introduction to Culture and Diversity

 READ in the text-book:

Chapter I   *A Different Mirror* by Ronald Takaki

Chapter II   *What Is Culture?* by Eugene Garcia

I. INTRODUCTION
In the first Program you will have the opportunity to become familiar with the students and instructor of this media Program. It is very important to understand our own cultural backgrounds and origins in order to help us understand the differences as well as the similarities among individuals and groups in our society. In order to accomplish this you will observe the media students participating in an exercise called "Who In The World Is In Here? Be sure to record the various backgrounds of each student on the attached forms so that you can make inferences about the diversity of the media students. For example, what geographic locations were most students' ancestors from? In addition, these perceptions will be compared against the DNA results a few of the students submitted to the National Geographic's Genographic Project.

We will also learn a number of key terms and definitions which will be necessary for you to understand in order to comprehend the material in this course. Be sure to use the glossary of terms at the back of the study guide.

II. VIDEO INSERTS
There are two videos for our first Program. The first insert is a video overview of some of the many cultures, issues, and groups we will explore in this course. As you watch consider the following questions:

1. Describe at least three cultures, issues, or groups presented in this opening video montage.

Learning how to value interracial communities + how to help them be stable", I saw young african boys, and asian people

2. Which segment was most interesting to you?

The patriarchy

3. Which segment was least interesting to you?

The second insert is a segment showing Dr. Adams preparing a DNA sample to be sent to the National Geographic's Genographic Project.

1. Hypothesize what you think Dr. Adams and the students will find out about their ancestry through this process.

2. What impact do you think scientific evidence like this will have on the way people think about race?

III. MEDIA GRAPHICS
Now watch Program 1.

IV. REVIEW QUESTIONS
Now that you have completed the reading and viewed the Program, answer the following questions to make sure you understand the key concepts presented.

1. What is your ethnic background? From what cultures do your ancestors come? To the best of your knowledge when did your first ancestors arrive in the Americas?

2. Compare some of the inferences the media Program students made with your own inferences from the "Who In The World Is In Here" exercise.

3. According to the article written by Garcia, define the key elements of the term "culture."

4. List some of the reasons that Takaki gives for why it is difficult for people in the United States of America to share a common identity.

5. Why does Takaki suggest that people in the U.S.A. need to see themselves in a "Different Mirror?"

V. SUGGESTED ADDITIONAL BACKGROUND MATERIALS
Books:
Takaki, G. (1993). A Different Mirror: A History of America. Boston: Little Brown and Company.
Zinn, Howard (2003). A People's History of the United States. New York: Harper Collins Publishers Inc.

Journals:
Multicultural Perspectives, Lawrence Erlbaum Associates, Inc., Mahwah, NJ (J).

Internet Websites:
National Association of Multicultural Educators (NAME) www.nameorg.org
The Genographic Project   www.nationalgeographic.com/genographic

VI. KEY VOCABULARY TERMS

Hypo descent *one drop of african american or other blood you are that.*
Ethnicity
Cultural identity
Culture *Coa...*
Macro-culture
Micro-culture
Paradigm
Social construction
Ethnic group
Race
Ethnocentrism
Social mobility system
Patriarchy
Hegemony
DNA

VII. SUPPLEMENTARY MATERIALS

Who In The World Is In Here?

List the ethnic backgrounds of each Program participant:

List the religious/spiritual backgrounds of each Program participant:

List the size of the community in which each of the Program participants grew up:

Dealing With Diversity — Program 2
Social Interaction Model

 READ in the text-book:

Chapter 3. *Understanding Social Interaction in the 21st Century* by J. Q. Adams.

I. INTRODUCTION
In this Program you will learn to use a social interaction model (SIM) that will help shape your understanding of how humans interact in culturally diverse settings. This model has five major components that are overlapping and interdependent upon each other. The vocabulary which we will introduce to you is critical for our discussions in all the remaining Programs in this course. In essence, this model and its vocabulary will give us a common language and construct with which we can describe and explore the various issues we will encounter in this course.

II. VIDEO INSERTS
The video insert for this Program is a scene taken from the film "Crash," the 2005 Academy Award winning film of the year. As you watch this scene, consider the following questions.

1. How does the propriospect of the participants in this scene affect the outcome?

2. Which type of event is characterized by this scene?

3. Describe the decision making component of the SIM in this scene.

4. What role does event familiarity play in this scene?

5. Why is social distance so critical to the interactions taking place in this event?

III. MEDIA GRAPHICS

Now watch Program 2.

IV. REVIEW QUESTIONS
Now that you have completed the reading and viewed the Program, answer the following questions to make sure you understand the key concepts presented.

1. Given your understanding of the SIM, describe any contemporary event in your recent experience at work, home, or at play.

2. How does the setting in which an event takes place affect the interaction of the participants?

3. Discuss how the SIM could help create greater understanding in a pluralistic society.

V. SUGGESTED ADDITIONAL BACKGROUND MATERIALS
Cushner, Kenneth (2003). *Human Diversity in Action: Developing Multicultural Competencies in the Programroom.* New York: McGraw-Hill.

Films:
Crash (2004). Director: Paul Haggis. Bob Yari Productions.

VI. KEY VOCABULARY

SIM's terms (see list)
MENSA

Dealing With Diversity — Program 3
Negotiating Cultural Communication

 READ in the text-book:

Chapter 4. *Intercultural Communication: A Current Perspective* by Milton J. Bennett.

I. INTRODUCTION

In this Program we will explore some of the varieties of communication styles that exist in the U.S.A as well as in other cultures around the world. To help you understand some of these styles our special in-Program guests are Isabel Lamptey (Great Britain), an educator from Western Illinois University and Michel Nguessan (Ivory Coast), a computer specialist at Governors State University. Both speak several different languages and have lived in a variety of countries around the world. This Program contains some audience participation activities. As you watch these staged greeting rituals, think about your own style and those that you have observed and/or experienced.

II. VIDEO INSERTS

The first video is an interview filmed in Malaysia with an interethnic couple, Asma Abdullah and Peter Shepherd. The interview discusses some of the cultural hurdles they have had to deal with in their marriage. As you watch this interview, consider the following questions:

1. Describe some of the problems that Asma and Peter face as a result of their cultural differences.

She sees him wearing less clothes to work in garden + feels like he needs more clothes

2. How have they learned to cope with these differences?

They learned to pick up on subtleties.

The second video is with Dr. Gordon Berry, Professor Emeritus at the University of California at Los Angeles (UCLA). Dr. Berry has consulted on numerous major Hollywood feature films as well as TV programs such as the Cosby Show. As you watch this interview, consider the following questions:

1. How does Hollywood perpetuate stereotypes in its feature films?

Its very stereo typed

2. Do minority writers help perpetuate stereotype to the same extent that majority writers do?

If they generally stick to the stereotypes.

III. MEDIA GRAPHICS
Now watch Program 3.

IV. REVIEW QUESTIONS

Now that you have completed the reading and viewed the Program, answer the following questions to make sure you understand the key concepts presented.

1. According to Bennett what is a "deviant" in intercultural education?

2. Identify and discuss at what stage you perceive yourself to be in terms of Bennett's model of Intercultural Sensitivity (ethnocentric to ethno-relative continuum).

3. What changes in your behavior would it take to move you to the next stage?

4. Explain the differences between a person using stereotypes rather than generalizations to describe the behavior of a group or person.

5. Describe some of the differences in the greeting rituals of the students who participated in the Program exercises.

6. Discuss some of the differences as well as similarities between the cultural greeting rituals of African versus Japanese cultures.

7. What is the difference between low context and high context cultures?

V. SUGGESTED ADDITIONAL BACKGROUND MATERIALS

Hofstede, Gert Jan & Pedersen, Paul B. (2002). *Exploring Culture: Exercises, Stories, and Synthetic Cultures.* Intercultural Press.

Hall, Edward T. (1974). *Handbook for Proxemic Research. Washington: Society for Anthropology of Visual Communication.*

Maggio, Rosalie (1997). *Talking About People: A Guide to Fair and Accurate Language.* The Oryx Press: Phoenix, AZ.

Films:
Higher Learner (1995). Director: John Singleton. Columbia Pictures.

VI. KEY VOCABULARY
Fictive kinship
High context cultures
Low context cultures
Proxemics
Global village

Dealing With Diversity — Program 4
The Changing Face of America and the World

 READ in the text-book:

Chapter 5. *Diversity and Multiculturalism on the Campus: How are Students Affected?* by Alexander Astin

Chapter 6. *Campus Resegregation and Its Alternatives* by Gary Orfield

I. INTRODUCTION

This Program concentrates on the rapidly changing demographic trends in the U.S.A. and around the world. In the first part of the Program we will examine the changing face of our country and learn about Wave Theory. Our in-studio guest is Michel Nguessan whose family is from the Ivory Coast of Africa. Michel grew up in a farm community and will share his experiences of living in a 2nd Wave Society. There will also be three video inserts that will allow us to examine the real impact these population changes have on our institutions and communities.

II. VIDEO INSERTS

There are three video inserts for this Program. The first is one of my favorites. It takes place in the Plaza De Los Angeles which is located in the urban center of Los Angeles, California. It is just a mere plaque, but on the plaque is inscribed the true essence of a young and diverse Southwest America. As you watch this short film segment, consider the following questions:

1. List the variety of ethnic groups listed on the plaque.

2. Why is this blend of ethnic diversity significant?

3. Discuss why it is not likely that you would find this kind of ethnic diversity on a historical marker on the east coast of the U.S.A.

The second video was filmed at UCLA. It includes a look at the students on campus and an interview with Dr. Alexander Astin.
1. Discuss the ethnic/racial backgrounds of the students you see in the video.

2. What does this tell us (if anything) about the possible/probable demographics of this part of California?

3. What were the major trends identified by Dr. Astin's annual research study?

4. Were you surprised by any of the findings in Dr. Astin's research?

The third video provides an overview of wave theory and illustrates each of the four stages.
1. Note the differences between each wave and the time it takes to progress from one wave to the next.

2. How does each wave influence education, family structure, work (how people make a living), and community?

3. What wave are you living in? Do you know anyone living in a different wave? Have you experienced living in a different wave?

III. MEDIA GRAPHICS

Now watch Program 4.

IV. REVIEW QUESTIONS
Now that you have completed the reading and viewed the Program, answer the following questions to make sure you understand the key concepts presented.

1. In which Wave does the vast majority of the world reside?

2. Describe the concept of "cultural shock" as people leave one Wave to live in another.

3. Discuss some of the consequences of this nation's changing demographics.

V. SUGGESTED ADDITIONAL BACKGROUND MATERIALS
Books:
Toffler, Alvin (1984) *The Third Wave*. Bantam: New York.
Denton, Nancy A. and Tolnay, Stewart E. (2002) *American Diversity: A Demographic Challenge for the Twenty-First Century*. State University of New York Press.

Internet Websites:
U.S. Census Bureau www.census.gov.

VI. KEY VOCABULARY
Demographics
Wave theory
Culture shock

Dealing With Diversity — Program 5
Immigration and the New Immigrants

 READ in the text-book:

Chapter 7.   *Building A Nation Through Immigration* by Edward Purcell

I. INTRODUCTION

This Program opens with a video of an immigration rally where we see large numbers of protesters speaking out about our country's policies on this controversial issue. In this Program we will consider the history of immigration laws in the U.S.A. We will begin by examining the immigration patterns in this country. We will also see several interviews beginning with Marian Smith of the Immigration and Naturalization Service (INS), White Racialist David Duke, and Marcelo Suarez, former director of Harvard University's Immigration Study. Our in-studio guest is Fred Tsao, Policy Director at the Illinois Coalition for Immigrant and Refugee Rights.

II. VIDEO INSERTS

The first video insert for this Program was filmed in Washington D.C. at the headquarters for the Immigration and Naturalization Service (INS). The interview is with Marian Smith, Chief Librarian at INS. As you watch this interview, consider the following questions:

1. What were some of the earliest immigration policies developed in the U.S.A?

2. Why were they developed?

3. Discuss some of the social sentiments that were being expressed by Americans at the end of the 19th and the beginning of the 20th century.

The second video insert contrasts three separate views on the immigration patterns taking place in this country. As you watch these interview segments, consider the following questions:

1. According to Suarez-Orozco what are the three major sources of immigration into the U.S.A?

2. What percentage of foreign born U.S. residents come from Mexico?

3. Discuss some of the fears expressed by David Duke in his interview. To what extent do you feel these fears are justified?

4. Explain what Munoz meant when he said that people in the U.S.A. have been victimized by an education that is largely Eurocentric and a-historical.

5. What group in America is the most diverse?

II. MEDIA GRAPHICS
Now watch Program 5.

III. REVIEW QUESTIONS
Now that you have completed the readings and viewed the Program, answer the following questions to make sure you understand the key concepts presented.

1. Briefly summarize the immigration patterns of the 19th and 20th centuries.

2. What forces encouraged the large scale migrations to North America?

3. Discuss the feelings of citizens in the U.S.A. at the end of the 19th century about the new immigrant populations coming into the country.

4. Describe some of the current attitudes toward immigration in this country.

5. Identify some of the problems immigrants in the U.S.A have bringing their relatives to this country as a result of our current immigration laws.

IV. SUGGESTED ADDITIONAL BACKGROUND MATERIALS
Books:

Duke, David (1998). *My Awakening.* Free Speech Press: Covington, LA.
Lerner, W and Sloan, J. (2003). *Crossing the Boulevard: Strangers, Neighbors, Aliens in New America.* New York: Norton & Company, Ltd.

Internet Websites:
The International Center for Migration, Ethnicity, and Citizenship www.newschool.edu/icmec/
U.S. Immigration and Naturalization Service (INS) www.ins.usdoj.gov

V. KEY VOCABULARY
Racialist
Stereotypes
Generalization
Xenophobia
Jingoism

Dealing With Diversity — Program 6
Race: The World's Most Dangerous Myth

 READ in the text-book:

Chapter 8. *Racial Identity and the State: The Dilemmas of Programification* by Michael Omi.

I. INTRODUCTION
This Program explores one of our nation's most complex and pressing problems, the concept and use of race. Deeply rooted in our historical past, this concept has multiple meanings for each and every one of us. The significance lies deep in our socialization/enculturation and is manifested as much in the educational curriculum as it is in the societal curriculum.

II. VIDEO INSERTS
There are two video interviews with Dr. Michael Omi, Professor of Ethnic Studies at the University of California at Berkeley. Listen closely as he discusses the changes in our society's view of race and how we now define and use the term. As you watch these interviews, consider the following questions:

1. How has popular culture changed the meaning of race in the U.S.A.?

2. Does a racial hierarchy exist in the U.S.A.? If you think it does, describe this hierarchy.

3. Discuss the difficulties Euro-Americans have with ethnic Americans who are not from a European cultural background.

III. MEDIA GRAPHICS
Now watch Program 6.

IV. REVIEW QUESTIONS

Now that you have completed the reading and viewed the Program, answer the following questions to make sure you understand the key concepts presented.

1. According to Omi, how has the concept of "race" changed over the last decade?

2. Discuss the difference between race and ethnicity.

3. Why "race" is considered our most dangerous myth?

4. How do our eyes deceive us about the issue of "race?"

5. Why do Americans tend to over estimate the number of interracial marriages in the U.S.A.?

V. SUGGESTED ADDITIONAL BACKGROUND MATERIALS

Books:

West, Cornell (1994). *Race Matters*. Auburn, CA: The Audio Partners Publishing Corp. Book on cassette.

Articles:

Gould, Stephen J. (2008). "Geometer of Race". Annual Editions. Dubuque, IA.

Internet Websites:

Supreme Court Legal Information Institute http://supct.law.cornell.edu/supct/index.html

Patterns of Variability: The Concept of Race.
www.as.ua.edu/ant/bindon/ant101/lectures/race/race1.htm

VI. KEY VOCABULARY

Race
One drop rule
Social construction

Dealing With Diversity — Program 7
Social Class Issues

 READ in the text-book:

Chapter 9. **Discrimination** by Richard T. Schaefer

I. INTRODUCTION
In this Program we will look at the impact of social economics on the lives of families and individuals in the U.S.A. We will focus on "homelessness" and the phenomenon of "white flight" that is occurring in many neighborhoods and communities across the country. Our in-studio guests are Linzey Jones, Mayor of Olympia Fields, and Don DeGraff, Mayor of South Holland, Illinois. Both of our guests will help us understand "white flight" by sharing their experiences of the causes and remedies to this unique social problem.

II. VIDEO INSERTS
The first video insert is a case study examining homelessness and its impact on individuals and families. As you watch the case-study, consider the following questions:

1. What are the reactions of pedestrians as they walk past the homeless people in the video insert? Would you be likely to react the same way?

2. Listen closely to the Janice Grady interview; how does she describe her feelings about being homeless and living on the streets?

3. According to Mike Meehan from the Center for Creative Non-Violence (CCNV), who is most likely to become homeless in the U.S.A.?

The second video insert is an interview with Dr. Gary Orfield, Harvard University researcher and public policy analyst. As you watch the interview, consider the following questions:

1. List the three kinds of racial inequality that have taken place in this country.

2. Why does Orfield believe that the suburbs will be the next great area of migration for African Americans and those of Latino origin?

3. What might be the reaction of white homeowners to a large influx of African Americans and Latinos in their neighborhoods and communities?

The third video insert is a case study of "white flight" in the southern suburbs of Chicago. As you watch the case-study, consider the following questions:

1. How does social Program play a role in "white flight?"

2. What is the reaction of the business community to "white flight?"

3. Discuss some of the mythology that drives "white flight."

4. How is it that cities like South Holland were successful in stabilizing their communities when others around them have failed?

III. MEDIA GRAPHICS
Now watch Program 7.

IV. REVIEW QUESTIONS
Now that you have completed the reading and viewed the Program, answer the following questions to make sure you understand the key concepts presented.

1. Discuss the different types of discrimination identified by Schaefer.

2. According to Schaefer what are the two main methods of reducing discrimination in the U.S.A.?

3. Which social class is most affected by formal education?

4. Why are African Americans more affected by the intersections of race and Program than other groups in American society?

5. Discuss the concepts of "glass ceiling" and "glass walls" as described by Schaefer.

V. SUGGESTED ADDITIONAL BACKGROUND MATERIALS
Orfield, Gary (1995). "Housing and the Justification of School Segregation," *University of Pennsylvania Law Review.* Vol. 143 Issue: n5 pp. 1397-1406.
Schaefer, Richard (2007) *Racial and Ethnic Groups.* 11th ed. Prentice Hall, New York.

Internet Websites:
People Like Us: Social Class in America   www. cnam.com

Films:
People Like Us: Social Class in America (2001). Director: Louis Alvarez and Andrew Kolker. New York: The Center for New American Media.

VI. KEY VOCABULARY
White flight
Glass ceiling
Glass walls

Dealing With Diversity — Program 8
Gender Issues

 READ in the text-book:

Chapter 10. *Interactive Phases of Curricular Revision: A Feminist Perspective* by Peggy McIntosh.

Chapter 11. *A Feminist's Silver Screen Scan: Where Have All the Women Gone?* by Janice Welsch.

I. INTRODUCTION
This Program examines the multiple dimensions of gender in our society. We will first examine the role of women and the difficulties they face gaining equity in a patriarchal society. In contrast to our discussions on women we will preview two segments from Byron Hurt's film, Hip Hop: Beyond Beats and Rhymes that examines the misogyny and violence personified in Hip Hop music and culture.

II. VIDEO INSERTS
The first media segment for this Program is Part I of an interview with Wellesley College Professor Peggy McIntosh. As you watch this interview, consider the following questions:

1. What was the difficulty that McIntosh encountered with her male counterparts at Wellesley College?

2. Discuss the evolvement of McIntosh's views about racism and sexism.

3. Why is the concept of unearned privilege so important for Americans to understand? Why is it so difficult for those who have it to recognize it?

The second media roll-in is a segment from Byron Hurt's documentary film that critiques some of the controversial elements found in the lyrics and images of Hip Hop culture's music and videos. As you watch this film clip consider the following questions:

1. List some of the reasons given by Hip Hop artists for the use of violent images in their music and videos.

2. In your opinion does this justify the use of these images?

The third media roll-in is another segment from Byron Hurt's film **Hip Hop: Beyond Beats and Rhymes.** As you watch this film clip consider the following questions:

1. What needs to happen to change the images found in most Hip Hop products?

2. Discuss what you like and/or dislike about Hip Hop.

3. Why do you think young women participate in the Hip Hop culture even when they are being sexually objectified?

The fourth interview continues with Dr. McIntosh discussing how students can use their advantages to support change on their campuses and in their communities.

1. Discuss some of the strategies "White" students can use to empower individuals who have not traditionally had power.

2. What might the privileged student earn from learning to share the power in society?

III. MEDIA GRAPHICS

Now watch Program 8.

The graphics you will see on the screen are reproduced below to save you the trouble of copying them down. You might like to add your own comments as you watch the tape.

IV. REVIEW QUESTIONS
Now that you have completed the reading and viewed the Program, answer the following questions to make sure you understand the key concepts presented.

1. Why is McIntosh concerned about educators' ability to re-see or re-shape the traditional curriculum in our schools?

2. What can people of privilege do to assist people who suffer from unearned disadvantages?

3. Do you think Hip Hop has the ability to change its image and become more sensitive to issues of violence and sexuality?

4. How much change has taken place in the last 100 years for women in occupations in the U.S.A?

5. Who benefited most from the 1965 Civil Rights Act?

V. SUGGESTED ADDITIONAL BACGROUND MATERIALS
Books:
Hooks, Bell (2000). *Feminist Theory: From Margin to Center.* South End Press: Boston, MA.

Dyson, Michael E. (2007). *Know What I Mean: Reflection on Hip-Hop.* Basic Civitas Books: New York.

Internet Websites:
National Organization of Women (NOW) www.now.org

Films:
Hip-Hop: Beyond Beats & Rhymes (2006). Director: Byron Hurt. Northampton, MA: Media Education Foundation.

VI. KEY VOCABULARY
Feminism
Hyper-masculinity
Misogyny
Patriarchy
Desentization

Dealing With Diversity — Program 9
Native Americans

 READ in the text-book:

Chapter 12. *Civic Literacy, Sovereignty, and Violence: Ojibwe Treaty Rights and Racial Backlash in the North Country* by Gaetano B. Senese.

I. INTRODUCTION
In this Program we will explore a variety of issues facing Native American cultures in the U.S.A. Our in-studio guest is Joseph (Standing Bear) Schranz, an Ojibwa from the Midwest Soaring Foundation. We also will see a variety of video inserts examining cultural identity, sovereignty, and education.

II. VIDEO INSERTS
The first video insert shows a Pow Wow of the Ho Chunk Nation. As you watch this celebration, consider the following questions:

1. Describe the activities taking place at the Pow Wow.

2. How is this activity different or similar to celebrations in your culture?

The second video insert focuses on the complex issues of treaty rights and sovereignty. Native American as well as Euro-American educators from Northern Arizona University are our informants. As you watch these interviews, consider the following questions:

1. What is the legal status of Navajo people in the U.S.A?

2. Why is sovereignty so important to Native American people?

The third video insert features several Native Americans discussing the problems of cultural identity and the strategies of assimilation versus acculturation. As you watch these interviews, consider the following questions:

1. Discuss the difficulty of avoiding the tag, "Red Apple." Why are people like John Wilmer vulnerable to being perceived in this manner?

2. Contrast your experience of coming to college for the first time with that of Native Americans who grew up in a traditional family.

3. According to Joe Martin why do so many young Native Americans leave the reservation and not return once they get their college educations?

The fourth video insert is a case study of Little Singer Community School (LSCS), a Charter School located on a Navajo Reservation 50 miles outside of Flagstaff, Arizona. As you watch this case study, consider the following questions:

1. Describe the physical landscape of the Navajo reservation surrounding Little Singer Community School (LSCS).

2. What characteristics make LSCS different from other schools?

3. Discuss in your own words why Native Americans are so passionate about maintaining their traditional cultures.

III. MEDIA GRAPHICS
Now watch Program 9.

IV. REVIEW QUESTIONS
Now that you have completed the reading and viewed the Program, answer the following questions to make sure you understand the key concepts presented.

1. Explain some of the differences between what you learned in school about Native Americans versus the information you have learned in this Program.

2. Why do Native Americans have to continue to struggle for the basic civil rights accorded to them by treaties signed with the United States of America's government?

3. What is the danger Joseph Standing Bear warns about regarding the wealth some Native American groups are receiving as the result of the profits coming from their gambling casinos?

V. SUGGESTED ADDITIONAL BACGROUND MATERIALS
Books:
Josephy, Alvin, M. (2005). *500 Nations*. Pimlico: Wild West.

Banks, Dennis and Erdoes (2004). *Obibwa Warrior: Dennis Banks and the Rise of the American Indian Movement.* Norman: University of Oklahoma Press.

Deloria, Vine (1988). *Custer Died for your Sins: An Indian Manifesto.* Norman: University of Oklahoma Press.

Internet Websites:
American Indian Science and Engineering Society (AISES) http://spot.colorado.edu/~aises/aises.html

VI. KEY VOCABULARY
Sovereignty
Red Apple
Traditional cultures
Pow-Wow

Dealing With Diversity — Program 10
Latino Americans, Part 1

READ in the text-book:

Chapter 13. *Latina/os Achieving Success* by Jeanette Castellanos

Chapter 14. *The Cultural Patterning of Achievement Motivation: A Comparison of Mexican, Mexican Immigrant, Mexican America, and Non-Latino White American Students* by Marcelo Suarez-Orozco and Carola E. Suarez-Orozco.

I. INTRODUCTION

This is the first of two Programs on Latino Americans. We will attempt to understand the variety of cultural groups that are Programified under these labels and also why they are projected to soon be the largest ethnic group in our country. There are four video inserts for this Program. Our in-studio guest is Rey Flores, a community activist and columnist for Hoy Newspaper in Chicago.

II. VIDEO INSERTS

The opening video is a segment from the Ballet Folkloric filmed during a Mexican Independence Day celebration. As you watch this performance, consider the following questions:

1. Describe the features of the performers; what similarities or differences does this performance have compared to other dance performances you have seen before?

2. How do events like this add to the richness of the American culture?

The first video insert is an interview with Professor Carlos Munoz, Jr. at the University of California at Berkeley. Dr. Munoz challenges us to see Latinos through a non-traditional cultural lens. As you watch this interview, consider the following questions:

1. Why does Munoz refer to Latinos as indigenous people?

2. What are some of the implications of Latinos being considered an indigenous group?

The second video insert is an interview with Dr. Marcelo Suarez-Orozco, director of the Harvard Immigration program. As you watch this interview, consider the following questions:

1. Describe the differences between the immigration patterns at the beginning of the 20th century as compared to the beginning of the 21st century.

2. What creates the problem of "hyper-segregation" as described by Suarez-Orozco?

The third video insert is an interview with Janet Castellanos, a professor at the University of California at Riverside. In this interview she gives us a condensed overview of Latino cultural identity theory. As you watch this interview, consider the following questions:

1. Discuss the various stages of Latino cultural identity.

2. How could knowledge of this model aid professionals in understanding the behavior of Latinos?

The fourth video insert is Dr. Ronald Gallimore of the University of California at Los Angeles. Dr. Gallimore's research focuses on Latino children and their families' attitudes about education (Core Values).

1. According to the research conducted by Dr. Gallimore describe some of the differences exhibited by Latino parents as compared to Anglo parents in the U.S.

2. Discuss the significance of spirituality in the lives of Latino families.

III. MEDIA GRAPHICS
Now watch Program 10.

IV. REVIEW QUESTIONS
Now that you have completed the reading and viewed the Program, answer the following questions to make sure you understand the key concepts presented.

1. Name at least ten groups that are Programified under the term "Hispanic."

2. Why is it that some Hispanic/Latino groups have fared better economically and educationally than others?

3. According to the research by Gallimore and others, are Latino families more likely to value moral or educational values?

4. What are the implications of this research for educators?

V. SUGGESTED ADDITIONAL BACGROUND MATERIALS

Books:
Carger, Chris Liska (1996). *Of Borders and Dreams: A Mexican-American Experience of Urban Education.* Teachers College Press: New York.

Internet Websites:
Latino On-line News Network www.latin.com

VI. KEY VOCABULARY
Indigenous
Hyper-segregation

Dealing With Diversity — Program 11
Latino Americans, Part 2

 READ in the text-book:

Chapter 15.   Mapping Latino Studies by Antonio Darder

I. INTRODUCTION

In the second Program on Hispanic/Latino Americans we will welcome back our in-studio guest Rey Flores. Joining Mr. Flores is Chicago realtor/community activist Fred Medina. Together they will provide some unique insights into the variety of opinions in the Latino community. This Program also features a case study on the fast growing Latino community in Beardstown, Illinois, and some of the many challenges facing its new and older population. We will also examine the second film clip from the Academy Award winner "Crash" and a final clip from an interview with Prof. Janet Castellanos, of the University of California at Riverside. In this clip she discusses the impact of Latino culture on education.

II. VIDEO INSERTS

The opening video insert is of folk guitarist, Chuy Negrette, an ethno-historian who is singing about the history of Mexicans in the American experience. As you watch this performance, consider the following questions:

1. What did you find humorous or funny about the lyrics in Negrette's music?

2. Is the use of satire an effective way of teaching cultural history; why yes or why not?

The first video insert is a mini case study of Beardstown, a small river town in central Illinois with a rapidly growing Latino population. This case study contains a variety of interviews with both Latinos and Anglos examining the challenges of a new population in a small community.

1. Identify and describe some of the challenges facing the Latino community in Beardstown.

2. What are the reactions of the Anglo community to the large influx of Latinos into the community?

The second video insert is from the Academy Award winning film "Crash." As you watch this film clip, consider the following questions:

1. Using the SIM, evaluate the interaction that takes place in this scene.

2. Why do you think prejudice and stereotypes are so rampant in our society?

3. What do you think is the long-term impact of this type of discrimination on victims such as the lock-smith in this film clip?

In this final clip from an interview with Prof. Janet Castellanos, of the University of California at Riverside, she discusses the impact of Latino culture on education. As you watch, consider the following question:

1. How does your culture impact your view of the educational process?

III. MEDIA GRAPHICS
Now watch Program 11.

IV. REVIEW QUESTIONS
Now that you have completed the reading and viewed the Program, answer the following questions to make sure you understand the key concepts presented.

1. Did you agree or disagree with the opinions of Rey Flores and Fred Medina?

2. Do you think their views are representative of the general Hispanic/Latino population?

V. SUGGESTED ADDITIONAL BACGROUND MATERIALS

Flores-Gonzáles, N. (2002). *School Kids / Street Kids*. New York: Teachers College, Columbia University.

Delgado, R., and Stefancic J. (1998). *The Latino Condition.* New York: New York University Press.

Darder, Antonia and Torres, R. D. (2004). *After Race: Racism After Multiculturalism*. New York University Press: New York.

Films:
A Day Without A Mexican (2004). Director, Sergio Arau. Eye on the Ball Films.

My Family/Mi Familia (1994). Director, Gregory Nava. American Playhouse.

Internet Websites:
National Council of La Raza (NCLR) www.ncir.org

VI. KEY VOCABULARY
Red lining

Dealing With Diversity — Program 12
African Americans, Part 1

 READ in the text-book:

> Chapter 16. ***Nobody Knows My Name: In Praise of African Evaluators Who Were Responsive*** by Stafford Hood

> Chapter 17. ***U.S. News Media: A Content Analysis and Media Case Study*** by Pearlie Strother-Adams

I. INTRODUCTION
This is the first of two Programs on African American culture in the U.S.A. In this segment we will examine some of the historical challenges faced by African Americans. In our video inserts we visit the Birmingham Civil Rights Museum, hear Prof. V.P. Franklin, Professor of History and Education at UC-Riverside explain the Core Values of African American Culture. In addition, we will examine another film clip from the Academy Award winning film "Crash and watch an interview with psychologist Thomas Parham who will discuss the cultural identity problems within the African American community." Our special in-studio guest is the distinguished Congressional Representative from the 2nd District of Illinois, Jesse Jackson, Jr.

II. VIDEO INSERTS
The first video insert was filmed on location at the Birmingham Civil Rights Museum in Birmingham, Alabama. During the civil rights movement Birmingham was the center of some of the most violent events of that era, often referred to as Bombmingham. The Civil Rights Museum stands as a reminder to a hostile past and hopeful future. As you watch this case study, consider the following questions:

1. Describe some of the museum's exhibits and their significance in promoting a better understanding of the African American experience during the civil rights era.

2. What was the significance of the park sign that reads, "No Dogs and Cats Allowed!"?

The second video insert was an interview conducted with Dr. V.P. Franklin who explores the traditional Core Values of African American culture. As you watch this interview, consider the following question:

1. What insights did you gain about African American culture as the result of this interview?

The third video insert is a scene from the movie "Crash" in which we see a conversation between two of the characters, a white police officer and an African American business manager. As you watch this film clip, consider the following questions:

1. Use the SIM as a tool for examining the interaction you see between the two characters in the film clip.

2. In your opinion what is the director of the film trying to tell us about the repeated acts of bigotry and hatred depicted in the film?

The final video insert was an interview conducted with Dr. Thomas Parham in which he discusses aspects of Black Cultural Identity theory. As you watch this interview, consider the following questions:

1. What insights did you gain about African American people as the result of this interview?

2. Discuss the difficulty of maintaining a consistent identity that does not validate the core of one's African beginnings.

3. How will this information change the way you think and act among African American people?

III. MEDIA GRAPHICS
Now watch Program 12.

IV. REVIEW QUESTIONS

Now that you have completed the reading and viewed the Program, answer the following questions to make sure you understand the key concepts presented.

1. Using the data presented in this Program, briefly describe the current demographic characteristics of African Americans in the U.S.A.

2. State some reasons to support or deny the existence of discrimination against African-Americans and other groups in the U.S.A.

3. What recommendations did Congressional Representative Jackson have to improve the lives of African Americans?

4. According to the Congressman what do African Americans need to do to improve their own lives?

5. Recount and comment on the significance of Representative Jackson's birth date in the history of the civil rights era.

6. Why is "historical memory" subject to revision as generations go forward in time?

7. How does commercialism impact the will of young people to be part of the social action necessary to continue the quest for social justice, equality, and equity?

V. SUGGESTED ADDITIONAL BACGROUND MATERIALS

Parham, Thomas (2002). *Counseling Persons of African Descent: Multicultural Aspects of Counseling and Psychotherapy*. Sage Publications.

Hooks, Bell and Sheppard, Gilda (2006). *"Talking Trash: A Dialog About Crash."* www.allaboutbell.com/crash.

Films:
Malcolm X (1992). Director: Spike Lee. 40 Acres and a Mule Film Works.

Eyes on the Prize Part I & II (1986 & 1989). Producer: Harry Hampton. Blackside.

Internet Websites:
National Association for the Advancement of Colored People (NAACP) www.naacp.org

VI. KEY VOCABULARY

Apartheid
Jim Crow
Bombingham
Resiliency
Segregation

Dealing With Diversity — Program 13
African Americans, Part 2

 READ in the text-book:

Chapter 19. *Afrocentricity and Multicultural Education: Concept, Challenge and Contribution* by Maulana Karenga.

Chapter 20. *The Black Youth Project: The Attitudes and Behaviors of Young Black Americans Research Summary* by Cathy Cohen.

I. INTRODUCTION
In this second Program on African Americans we explore the more contemporary lives and challenges of "people of color" in the U.S.A. We will see excerpts from Byron Hurt's film "Hip Hop: Beyond Beats and Rhymes" which examines the impact of Hip Hop culture on African American youth culture. Our in-studio guests are Dr. Cathy Cohen and her graduate student Jamila Celestine-Michener from the University of Chicago. Dr. Cohen has just completed a research study exploring the beliefs of young African Americans in urban areas.

II. VIDEO INSERTS
The first video insert is an interview with Dr. Maulana Karenga, Professor of Black Studies at California State University, Long Beach. He is one of our nation's most distinguished scholars and the creator of the African American cultural holiday, "Kwanzaa." As you listen to his interview consider the following:

1. Why was the development of Kwanzaa important for the U.S. as well as the rest of the world?

2. What is the difference between Afrocentricity and Multicultural Education?

The second video insert for this class is a collection of several scenes taken from Byron Hurt's Hip Hop documentary Beyond Beats and Rhymes. As you watch these film clips, consider the following questions:

1. According to some of the Hip Hop artists in the film why is violence such an integral part of Hip Hop music and culture?

2. How has Hip Hop culture influenced contemporary African American society?

3. What changes are needed to bring Hip Hop back into the mainstream?

III. MEDIA GRAPHICS
Now watch Program 13.

IV. REVIEW QUESTIONS

Now that you have completed the reading and viewed the Program, answer the following questions to make sure you understand the key concepts presented.

1. How has Hip Hop influenced contemporary culture in the U.S.A.?

2. What insights did you gain from Byron Hurt's film?

3. List some of the findings from Dr. Cohen's research.

4. Are these findings consistent with the ideas in Byron Hurt's film?

V. SUGGESTED ADDITIONAL BACGROUND MATERIALS

Dyson, Michael E. (2000). *"Art, Commerce and Race: The Controversial Debate on Music and Violence."* The Committee on Commerce Science and Transportation. U.S. Senate. September 13, 2000.

Ogbu, J. (2003). *Black American Students in an Affluent Suburb: A Study of Academic Disengagement.* Mawah, New Jersey: Lawrence Erlbaum Associates.

Films:
Bamboozled (2000) Director: Spike Lee. 40 Acres and a Mule Film Works.
Baby Boy (2001) Director: John Singleton. Columbia Pictures.
Hip Hop Beyond Beats and Rhymes (2006) Director: Byron Hurt. Media Education Foundation.

KEY VOCABULARY
Hip Hop
MC
Hyper-masculinity
Misogyny

Dealing With Diversity — Program 14
Asian Americans

 READ in the text-book:

Chapter 21. *From Different Shores* by Ronald Takaki.

I. INTRODUCTION
In this Program we will examine some of the many cultures that fall under the label Asian Americans. We will begin with the dynamic forces behind current immigration policy that are fueling the fastest growth among any ethnic groups in our society. Our in-studio guests are Rui Kaneya, managing editor of the Chicago Reporter, and Tuyet Le, executive director of the Asian American Institute. We will also see several video inserts that will help us understand the wide variety of Asian cultural experiences.

II. VIDEO INSERTS
The first interview is with Dr. Michael Omi, Professor of Ethnic Studies at the University of California at Berkeley. Dr. Omi has conducted research in the area of racial Programification and identity. As you watch the interview, consider the following questions:

1. Discuss the significance of some of the Supreme Court decisions on the status of racial privilege for Asian Americans.

2. How has our post 9/11 world affected the identity status of Asian Americans in our country?

The second video insert contains segments of interviews with Dr. Farah Ibrahim, Asma Abdullah and Peter Shepherd, and Dr. Gargi Roysircar-Sodowsky who will be discussing Asian cultural tradition. As you watch the interview, consider the following questions:

1. Discuss the concept of "saving face" and how it might influence Asian American behavior in the work place.

2. In Asian culture does "yes" always mean "yes" and "no" always "no"?

3. Are there any "Pan-Asian" cultural traits?

The third video insert is a case study of the Korean American community in Chicago. As you watch the interview, consider the following questions:

1. Discuss some of the "Push-Pull" factors that influenced the decisions of Koreans to migrate to this country.

2. What are some of the strong cultural values that still dominate the Korean community in this country?

3. How do these strong cultural values conflict with the ideas of the young American-born Koreans?

4. What are some of the solutions to the conflicts between the Korean American business community and the African American communities their businesses serve?

MEDIA GRAPHICS
Now watch Program 14.

III. REVIEW QUESTIONS
Now that you have completed the reading and viewed the Program, answer the following questions to make sure you understand the key concepts presented.

1. Why do people of color have difficulty with their identity regardless of how long they have been in this country?

2. Discuss whether "Asians as Model Minorities" is myth or fact within the American society.

3. Describe some of the cultural differences between Asian, African, and European American communities.

IV. SUGGESTED ADDITIONAL BACGROUND MATERIALS
Books:
Takaki, Ronald (1994). From Different Shores: Perspectives on Race and Ethnicity in America. 2nd Edition. New York: Oxford University Press.

Film:
The Joy Luck Club (1993) Director: Wayne Wong. Hollywood Pictures.

Who Killed Vincent Chin? (1988) Director & Producer: Renee Tajima & Christine Choy.

Internet Websites:
Asian American Resources www.ai.mit.edu/people/irie/aar/
Asian American Studies Center www.aasc.ucla.edu/default.asp
Asian-Nation www.asian-nation.org/index.shtml

V. KEY VOCABULARY
Saving face
Immigration Wave Theory

Dealing With Diversity — Program 15
Middle Eastern and Arab Culture

 READ in the text-book:

Chapter 22. *Reel Bad Arabs* by Dr. Jack Shaheen

I. INTRODUCTION

This is the first of two Programs on Middle Eastern, Arab, and Islamic cultures in the U.S.A. In the first Program we will view several scenes from Dr. Jack Shaheen's film "Reel Bad Arabs," an exploration of the images of Arabs in Hollywood films. Our in-studio guest is Ahmed Rehab, Executive Director of the Council on American-Islamic Relations (CAIR) in Chicago.

II. VIDEO INSERTS

In the first video insert we see a montage of Arab and Islamic images in the media. As you watch these images, consider the following questions:

1. What do you think of when you see images of Arabs?

2. When you think of Arab religions what do you think about?

3. Why have these images become so negative in the American public's eye?

In the second video insert we see some scenes from Jack Shaheen's documentary film "Reel Bad Arabs." This is the follow up to his highly respected book of the same name that examines the history of Hollywood films and how they have depicted Arab people and culture. As you watch these film clips, consider the following questions:

1. What characteristics are consistently evident in the film clips in this documentary?

2. Why do you think Hollywood film makers constantly use this line of film making?
In the third video insert we see another clip from Dr. Shaheen's documentary "Reel Bad Arabs."
As you watch these scenes, consider the following questions:

1. How does long term viewing of such images impact the American people's ideas about a people or culture?

2. Discuss the value of this form of social criticism for maintaining freedom of speech and information in our society.

III. MEDIA GRAPHICS
Now watch Program 15.

IV. REVIEW QUESTIONS
Now that you have completed the reading and viewed the Program, answer the following questions to make sure you understand the key concepts presented.

1. In your opinion how has Hollywood's long-term negative depictions of Arab and Middle Eastern cultures impacted the American people?

2. If Dr. Shaheen's assessment is true, how do we go about bringing a revised opinion of Arab people and cultures to the American public?

3. Were you surprised that over twenty million Christians live in the Middle East? Why or Why not?

4. Describe the Arab community in Chicago.

5. Can you think of any movies or programs in which there are positive Arab characters?

6. List some of the Arab values discussed in this Program.

V. SUGGESTED ADDITIONAL BACKGROUND MATERIALS

Books:
Shaheen, Jack (2006). Reel Bad Arabs: How Hollywood vilifies a people. New York: Olive Branch Press.

Internet Websites:
Council On American-Islamic Relations www.cairchicago.org

VI. KEY VOCABULARY
Propaganda
Yellow journalism
Islam phobia

Dealing With Diversity — Program 16
Islam

 READ in the text-book:

Chapter 23. *Islam, Muslims, and U.S. Media.* By Mohammad Siddiqi.

I. INTRODUCTION
In this Program we will focus on the fastest growing religion in the U.S.A and the world. We have our special in-studio guests Imam Kifah Mustapha (from the Bridgeview Mosque) who is also the Associate Director of The Mosque Foundation and Dr. Aminah Beverly McCloud, a professor of Islamic and Religious Studies at DePaul University, and Ahmed Rehab, the Executive Director of CAIR . There are several video inserts of Muslims practicing and discussing their faith around the world.

II. VIDEO INSERTS
The opening video montage takes a short look at Muslim culture. Pay close attention to the images that may be different from what you have seen in the past.

In the first video insert we see a short case study on the Islamic community in Waukegan, Illinois. In the video you will see the Waukegan Mosque and watch interviews with a variety of Muslims who live in the community.

1. Describe the variety of backgrounds of the Muslims represented in the interviews who are serving in the communities where they live.

2. What did you learn from this short case study about Muslims in Waukegan?

In the second video insert we see an interview with Dr. Azizan Baharuddin from the Centre for Civilizational Dialogue at the University of Malaysia. As you watch this interview, consider the following questions:

1. How is the meaning of Islam discussed in this interview different from the interpretation usually depicted in American media?

2. Does her dress/attire influence how you hear what she is saying?

In the final video insert we continue the interview with Dr. Baharuddin and several other Muslim women who talk about their faith. As you watch these interviews, consider the following questions:

1. Contrast the different views of these three women on Islam.

2. Are there any ideas in these interviews that are similar to your own religious/spiritual beliefs?

III. MEDIA GRAPHICS
Now watch Program 16.

IV. REVIEW QUESTIONS
Now that you have completed the reading and viewed the Program, answer the following questions to make sure you understand the key concepts presented.

1. In your opinion what are some of the differences as well as similarities between Christianity and Islam?

2. Approximately how many Muslims are there in the world?

3. What are some of things Dr. McCloud thought Americans should know about Muslims in the U.S.A?

4. What did you learn about Islam that you didn't know prior to this Program?

5. How has this information changed your opinion about Islam?

6. Where is the largest population of Muslims in the world?

7. Why was Dr. McCloud so critical of the map showing the locations of Muslims in the world?

8. Discuss some of the historical beginnings of negativity about Muslims in the U.S.A.

V. SUGGESTED ADDITIONAL BACGROUND MATERIALS
Books:

Barber, Benjamin (2003). *Jihad Vs. McWorld.* Corgi Books: Moorebank, NSW

Films:
Muslims (2002) Director: Graham Judd (Frontline).

Faith and Doubt at Ground Zero. (2002) Director: Whitney Helen. PBS Home Video.

VI. KEY VOCABULARY
Muslim
Islam
The Pillars of Islam
Sunni's
Shiites

Dealing With Diversity — Program 17
European Americans

 READ in the text-book:

Chapter 24. *Food and Italian American Identity in Big Night* (1996) by Roberta Di Carmine.

I. INTRODUCTION
European Americans are the focus of this Program. We have one of the most fascinating video case studies in the series that samples the cultures of the Amish and Mennonites in the U.S.A. In addition, our in-studio guest is historian and film maker Dominic Candeloro who will share his experiences as well as clips from his film And They Came to Chicago: The Italian American Legacy. At the end of the Program we will see the genetic trail of students and staff from the Genographic project in which the Program has participated.

II. VIDEO INSERTS
The first video is an exploration of Amish culture and their adaptation to a modern 4th Wave society like the U.S.A. As you watch it, consider the following questions:

1. When and why did the Amish settle in the U.S.A.?

2. What are some of the characteristics of the Amish community? How does this differ from other communities in our country?

3. Describe the rights of passage for young people in the Amish community.

4. Give an example of how Amish communities from across the country support each other.

5. Could you live in a community like this? Why or why not?

In the second video insert we will see a clip from the film, ***And They Came To Chicago: The Italian Americans Legacy*** (2007). As you watch the film clip, consider the following questions:

1. Discuss some of the prejudices Italian Americans encountered as they adapted to life in this country.

2. What did most Italian Americans believe was the ticket for success in the U.S.A.?

3. Explain the importance of family in the Italian heritage.

III. MEDIA GRAPHICS
Now watch Program 17.

IV. REVIEW QUESTIONS
Now that you have completed the reading and viewed the Program, answer the following questions to make sure you understand the key concepts presented.

1. Why do the Amish reject modernity?

2. In what wave do the Amish primarily live?

3. What are some of the challenges Italians face in maintaining their culture and heritage in this country?

4. Discuss the impact of the media's version of the Mafia and its influence on the average Italian American.

5. Describe some of the reasons Italian immigrants encountered so much prejudice when they first arrived in this country.

6. Why is the Italian American family so strong in America?

7. How has the church played a role in the lives of Italian Americans?

8. Discuss the significance of WWII to the integration of Italian Americans in the U.S.A.

9. What did you find interesting about the results of the DNA testing we did in Program?

V. SUGGESTED ADDITIONAL BACKGROUND MATERIALS

Film:
And They Came To Chicago: The Italian Americans Legacy (2007). Modio Media.

Devil's Playground (2002) Director: Lucy Walker. Cinemax Real Life.

VI. KEY VOCABULARY
Birds of paradise
Opera Singers
Amish
Mennonites
Rumspringa
Little Italy

Dealing With Diversity — Program 18
Creole and Mixed Ethnic Americans

 READ in the text-book:

Chapter 25. *The Americanization of Black New Orleans, 1850-1900*
by Joseph Logsdon and Caryn Cosse Bell

I. INTRODUCTION
This Program will examine the phenomenon of ethnic blending and what happens to individuals when they intermarry with others of different ethnic groups. We will begin with a video insert that traces the origins the Creole culture in New Orleans and its subsequent impact on the U.S.A. The second interview is a fascinating example of an "inter-racial" couple, Diane and Reggie Alsbrook, who live off the grid in New Mexico. Our in-studio guest is Robin Tillmon, President of the Bi-racial Family Network (BFN) in the Chicago area and the child of an inter-racial marriage. Our in-audience guest is Eric Glenn, the product of a mixed-race couple who will share some of his life's experiences. Finally, we will examine more of the DNA results from our students in the Program.

II. VIDEO INSERTS
In this video insert we travel to New Orleans, LA, and interview the late Dr. Joseph Logsdon, an authority on the history of Creole culture. As you watch this interview, consider the following questions:

1. Discuss the difference between the popular and historical definitions of the term "Creole."

2. Describe some of the historical political events in which "Black Creoles" participated as part of their quest for equal rights and freedom.

3. Contrast the differences between the customs and cultures of "whites" and "blacks" in New Orleans versus other major cities in the U.S.A.

4. Describe the differences Logsdon believes exist between Southern and Northern Louisiana.

In the second video insert we visit Reggie and Diane Alsbrook, an inter-racial couple who have been married since the early 1970s. They share stories about some of the interesting experiences they have had over the years.

1. Discuss some of the racial problems the Alsbrooks encountered as an "inter-racial" couple in the 1970s and 80s.

2. How did their "race" affect their business and/or professional experiences?

3. According to the experiences of the Alsbrooks, how much has changed in the last twenty-five years with regard to social relationships for "inter-racial" people?

III. MEDIA GRAPHICS
Now watch Program 18.

IV. REVIEW QUESTIONS
Now that you have completed the reading and viewed the Program, answer the following questions to make sure you understand the key concepts presented.

1. Why do we call New Orleans "the Big Easy?"

2. What makes New Orleans different than any other city in the U.S.A.?

3. Describe some of the characteristics that make jazz unique and speculate why New Orleans would be the birth place of this unique musical style.
4. Discuss some of the historical contributions that Black Creoles made to the freedom efforts of African American people in the U.S.A.?

5. Why are most estimates of the number of "inter-racial" couples consistently over estimated?

6. What does it mean to live "off the grid?"

7. How did the BFN get started? What benefits does it provide its members?

8. In your opinion why have race relations been so slow in improving in the U.S.A.?

V. SUGGESTED ADDITIONAL BACKGROUND MATERIALS
Films:
The Human Stain (2003) Director: Robert Benton. Miramax Films.

Lone Star (1996) Director: John Sayles. Columbia Pictures.

Mr. and Mrs. Loving (1996) Director: Richard Friedenberg. Daniel Paulson Films.

Internet Websites:
Human Rights Web   www.hrweb.org

VI. KEY VOCABULARY
Creole
Miscengation
Plessey v Ferguson
Jim Crow
French Quarter
Jazz
Zydeco

Dealing With Diversity ---- Program 19
Ethnocentric Groups in the USA

 READ in the text-book:

Chapter 26. *The Evolution of Race* by David Duke

Chapter 27. *Contingency, Irony, and Solidarity: A Moral of Multicultural Education* by James LaPrad.

I. INTRODUCTION

The social interaction of ethnic/racial groups in post-9/11 America sometimes lead to heated debates on whether different groups should live, work, marry, or go to school together. Decisions about immigration concern many Americans. This Program will explore the width and breadth of these debates from those who oppose integration to those who fight against bigotry and discrimination. This Program has four video interviews with activists from a variety of very different but very dedicated positions. We will hear from leaders at the Southern Poverty Law Center (SPLC) and see a segment from the HBO documentary film, Hate.Com: Extremists on the Internet. We will also hear from David Duke, a racialist with international connections and Leibe Geft, a leader at the Simon Wiesenthal Museum of Tolerance.

II. VIDEO INSERTS

In the first video insert we see representatives from the SPLC talk about the history, struggles, and accomplishments of the SPLC in Montgomery, Alabama. As you watch this video, consider the following questions:

1. What are some of the goals of the SPLC?

2. List some of the accomplishments of the SPLC.

3. Is there a "typical profile" of a person who would likely be involved in a "hate group?"

4. Who are the people targeted by "hate groups" in the U.S.A?

The second interview features David Duke who identifies himself as a "white racialist" or as a person who loves his own group. Duke has run and held public office in the state of Louisiana and unsuccessfully ran for the U.S. Congress. As you watch this interview, consider the following questions:

1. What are some of the concerns that Duke has about our current immigration policy in the U.S.A?

2. Discuss Duke's views on forced amalgamation?

3. According to Duke can different "races/ethnic groups" live civically together?

The third video insert is a film clip from a documentary film developed for HBO by the SPLC called, Hate .Com: Extremists on the Internet. This film chronicles the extent of hate websites available on the Internet. As you watch this film clip, consider the following questions:

1. Why do you think these websites are so dedicated to their beliefs?

2. How did the website of the teenage white racialist affect you?

The fourth video insert is a case study of the The Simon Wiesenthal Museum of Tolerance in Los Angeles, California. It honors the resiliency of the Jews and other ethnic groups that suffered through the tyranny of the Nazis during the Second World War and the fame of the celebrated Nazi hunter for whom the Museum is named.

1. Why was this Center and Museum created?

2. Who is T.J. Liedan, and what role does he play at the Center?

3. What kinds of actions can each of us take to improve the socio/cultural relationships in our neighborhoods and communities?

III. MEDIA GRAPHICS
Now watch Program 19.

IV. REVIEW QUESTIONS
Now that you have completed the reading and viewed the Program, answer the following questions to make sure you understand the key concepts presented.

1. List and discuss the basic characteristics of most ethnocentric groups.

2. Do you believe that ethnocentrism is just a by-product of different groups living in the same society? Why or why not?

3. Everyone has some ethnocentric views, describe yours.

4. Examine whether or not Duke's view is ethnocentric. Cite at least two examples from his chapter in the Anthology.

V. SUGGESTED ADDITIONAL BACGROUND MATERIALS
Films:

The Birth of A Nation (1915). Director: D. W. Griffith. D. W. Griffith Productions.

American History X (1998). Director: Tony Kaye. New Line Cinema.

Malcom X (1992). Director: Spike Lee. 40 Acres and a Mule.

Internet Websites:
Southern Poverty Law Center www.splcenter.org

VI. KEY VOCABULARY
Racialist
Bigot
Separatist
Amalgamation
Skin

Dealing With Diversity — Program 20
Sexual Orientation

 READ in the text-book:

Chapter 28. *Opening Programroom Closets: Teaching about Lesbians, Gay Men, and Bisexuals in a Multicultural Context* by Jovita Baber and Brett Beemyn

Chapter 29. *Our Daughters and Sons: Questions and Answers for Parents of Gay, Lesbian, and Bisexual People.* PFLAG

I. INTRODUCTION
There are an ever increasing number of gays, lesbians, bi-sexuals, and transsexuals who are coming out or are out. Many of these individuals are active in groups and organizations that are fighting to extend their rights in the public as well as private sectors. Our video insert is an interview with two gay and lesbian students from Emory University, located outside of Atlanta, Georgia. Our in-studio guests are Sylvia and Gysbert Menninga, parents of a gay child; Tamara McClatchey, a lesbian professional; and Dr. Alan Sanders, a researcher from the University of Chicago whose studies are attempting to understand if there is a genetic connection to homosexuality.

II. VIDEO INSERTS
None

III. MEDIA GRAPHICS
Now watch this media Program.

IV. REVIEW QUESTIONS
Now that you have completed the reading and viewed the Program, answer the following questions to make sure you understand the key concepts presented.

1. According to the article by Baber and Beemyn how is the media affecting the way people perceive Gay and Lesbian culture?

2. Why do Baber and Beemyn feel it is important to integrate Gay and Lesbian culture into the school curriculum?

3. Discuss the goals of Dr. Sanders' research.

4. If he is able to identify a gene for homosexuality, do you think it will change homophobic behavior in our society?

5. Do you think the general public will ever accept homosexual behavior in our country?

V. SUGGESTED ADDITIONAL BACKGROUND MATERIALS
Films:
Is it a Boy or Girl? (2000). Director: Phyllis Ward. The Intersex Society of North America.

Laramie Project (2002). Director: Moses Kaufman. Cane/Gabay Productions.

Internet:
Parents Families Lesbian And Gay Students (PFLAG) www.pflag.org

VI. KEY VOCABULARY
Gay
Lesbian
Bi-sexual
Transgendered
Homophobic
Heterosexist
Queer
PFLAG

Dealing With Diversity — Program 21
Physical and Mental Ability Issues

 READ in the text-book:

Chapter 30. *Disability Deception* by JoAnn Collins

I. INTRODUCTION
This Program focuses on one of the fastest growing minority groups in our nation, people with a disability. Our discussion will include interviews with Hiram Zayas and Lenda Hunt. Our in-studio guest is Robin Sweeney, an Academic Support Counselor and one of her advisees, Marion Kaes, a student at GSU.

II. VIDEO INSERTS
The first interview is with Hiram Zayas, a consultant who helps businesses deal with issues of access and compliance with ADA.

1. What are your initial reactions when you see Hiram Zayas for the first time? After his interview, did your first opinion change?

2. Why is access so important in the lives of the disabled?

3. According to Zayas the disabled are just beginning to become aware of their political and economic potential. What are the likely outcomes of their increased participation in our society?

The second interview is with Lenda Hunt who has been a participant in all three editions of DWD. She is an effective spokesperson for the disabled throughout our state and region.

1. What does the term TAB mean?

2. How accurate is this acronym in American society?

3. How do you feel about interacting with people with disabilities?

III. MEDIA GRAPHICS

Now watch Program 21.

IV. REVIEW QUESTIONS

Now that you have completed the reading and viewed the Program, answer the following questions to make sure you understand the key concepts presented.

1. Why are schools seemingly so reluctant to provide accommodations and services to students with disabilities?

2. What strategies can parents of disabled students use to more effectively advocate for their children?

3. Why do you think able-bodied people routinely ignore the rights of the disabled (eg.: park in handicapped spaces, not give people in wheel chairs priority on elevators, not enforce ordinances requiring access to public places, etc.)?

V. SUGGESTED ADDITIONAL BACKGROUND MATERIALS
Films:

A Beautiful Mind (2001) Director: Ron Howard, Universal Pictures.

I Am Sam (2001) Director: Jessie Nelson. New Line Cinema

VI. KEY VOCABULARY
TAB
ADA
Handicapped

Dealing With Diversity — Program 22
Age Issues: From Young to Old

 READ in the text-book:

Chapter 31. *Breaking Down the Myths of Aging* by John Rowe and Robert Kahn

I. INTRODUCTION

Age issues from young to old will be examined in this session. We have a video case study that looks at Adult Day Care for seniors. Our in-studio guest is Sally Furhmann, Director of the Rich Township Senior Center, and Pat Klein, Youth Director for Richton Park's Youth and Family Center. Our guest in the audience is Kenneth Kramer, President of the Park Forest, IL Chapter of AARP.

II. VIDEO INSERTS

Program 22 opens with a montage of video clips that challenge age-old stereotypes about aging. When you hear someone talking about "seniors," do you picture the typical senior citizen stereotypes or are your images more like what you see in the clips?

Our video case study is from the first edition of DWD. It is an example of the new services that are being created to meet the demands of the baby boomers who constitute the largest percentage of senior citizens in this nation's history.

1. What advantages does the adult daycare alternative have over the traditional nursing home facility in the U.S.A.?

2. In your opinion how did the people appear in this case study? Did they appear to be happy and content or just going through the paces?

III. MEDIA GRAPHICS

Now watch Program 22.

IV. REVIEW QUESTIONS

Now that you have completed the reading and viewed the Program answer the following questions to make sure you understand the key concepts presented.

1. Discuss some of the problems that young people face in this country.

2. Contrast the problems of children with the problems of the aged.

3. Why does it seem that the problems of both the young and aged are low priorities for our nation's leaders?

4. List the six myths about aging as described by Rowe and Kahn.

5. Briefly discuss the evidence presented by Rowe and Kahn that disputes our nation's popular myths about aging.

V. SUGGESTED ADDITIONAL BACKGROUND MATERIALS
Books:
Rowe, John W. and Kahn, Robert L. (1998). *Successful Aging*. Pantheon Books.

Internet Websites:
Child Welfare League of America (CWLA) www.cwla.org

The Children's Defense Fund (CDF) www.cdf.org

VI. KEY VOCABULARY
AARP
Aged
Alzheimer's Disease

Dealing With Diversity — Program 23
The State of New South Africa

READ in the text-book:

Chapter 32. *Now That The TRC Is Over: Looking Back, Reaching Forward* by Charles Villa-Vicencio.

Chapter 33. *African Mysteries* by Patti Waldmeir

I. INTRODUCTION
This Program provides an update on the promising new democracy of The Republic of South Africa. Our video case study begins shortly before the second democratic election. Our in-studio guest is Machiel van Niekerk, Consul at the South African Consulate-General, Chicago

VIDEO INSERTS
The first video chronicles the triumphant return of Nelson Mandela as he leaves prison after 27 years of incarceration. We also see interviews with two significant participants during the early changes of government in SA: Wilmont James of the Institute for Democracy in South Africa (IDASA) and Charles Villa-Vicencio who worked for the Truth in Reconciliation Committee (TRC).

1. Describe the atmosphere of the crowds as Mandela is released from prison.

2. Why was this event so important to South Africans and to the world?

3. Villa-Vicencio stated that "the victims of apartheid do not have the luxury of forgetting." What do you think he meant by that?

4. Why does Wilmont James feel that part of the solution to inequities in South Africa must be an increase in educational spending for the previous victims of apartheid?

5. Why is there a feeling that South Africa is still two nations?

The second video insert gives us an insight into the life of a "colored" family. The interview shows glimpses of both their church and home life.

1. Contrast the church service in the case study to that of your own church/religious experience in the U.S.A.

2. Describe the changing perceptions that "Coloreds" have of "Blacks" in South Africa?

3. What visions of the future did the young people in the case study describe for themselves?

4. Describe the parable of the baboon as told by Rev. Weeder.

5. Discuss whether or not you believe the Gordon-Philander family is optimistic about their futures in this new South Africa.

6. How much hope did Rev. Weeder express about the children in his family and congregation?

In the third video insert we talk to students at Cecil B. Rhodes High School in South Africa.

1. Did the students share a common perspective on the conditions in South Africa?

2. What did the young students say about their cultural identity in the school and in the general society?

II. MEDIA GRAPHICS
Now watch Program 23.

III. REVIEW QUESTIONS

Now that you have completed the reading and viewed the Program, answer the following questions to make sure you understand the key concepts presented.

1. What are the three major Programifications of people in South Africa?

2. List some of the problems facing the people of South Africa in order to maintain their democracy.

3. Discuss Villa-Vicencio's views on the difficulty of achieving true national reconciliation in South Africa.

4. While the Consul from South Africa indicated the physical Apartheid ended in South Africa, the economic Apartheid still continues. Discuss why this has been so difficult to change.

5. Why did the TRC work so effectively and what were the consequences of not being truthful and forth coming?

6. What is the status of South Africa's economy in contrast to the rest of Africa?

IV. SUGGESTED ADDITIONAL BACKGROUND MATERIALS
Books:
Mandela, Nelson (1994). *Long Walk to Freedom: The Autobiography of Nelson Mandela*.
    Little Brown: New York.

Waldmeir, Patti (1998). *Anatomy of a Miracle*. Rutgers Press.

Films:
Long Night's Journey Into Day (2000). Directors: Deborah Hoffman & Frances Reid.

Catch A Fire (2006). Director: Philip Noyce. Mirage Enterprises.

Internet Websites:
Africa News Online www.africanews.org

V. KEY VOCABULARY
Apartheid
Coloreds
Bantu Stands
Townships

Dealing With Diversity — Program 24
Diversity Issues and Answers

 READ in the text-book:

Chapter 34. ***Chess Impacts My Life*** by Maurice Ashley.

Chapter 35. ***How Real is Race? Using Anthropology to Make Sense of Human Diversity*** by Carol Mukhopadhyay and Rosemary Henze.

I. INTRODUCTION
This is the final Program of DWD 3. It will provide a review of many of the essential topics we have explored. Our in-studio guest is Dr. Robert D. Martin, Curator of Anthropology at the Field Museum in Chicago. His research is in the development of primates which will help us understand some of the issues we have raised about race and the Genographic Project in which we have participated during this course.

We will also see a video interview with a representative of the Jehovah's Witnesses who speaks about their multicultural religious organization, and the International Chess Grandmaster Maurice Ashley who will share his stories about how he became the first African American to obtain this status.

II. VIDEO INSERTS
The first interview is with a representative of the Jehovah's Witnesses at their headquarters in New York.

1. Do you agree with the answer for getting along in a cultural milieu like the U.S.A.?

2. Why is this so difficult to achieve in our society?

The second video interview is with Maurice Ashley, the first African American International Grand Chess master in the world. He is also known for leading the Raging Rooks, a Junior High Chess team from Harlem, New York, to the national championship. As you watch this interview, consider the following questions:

1. How does Ashley believe chess helps young people in school?

2. What were some of the reasons Ashley became interested in chess?

III. MEDIA GRAPHICS
Now watch Program 24.

IV. REVIEW QUESTIONS
Now that you have completed the reading and viewed the Program, answer the following questions to make sure you understand the key concepts presented.

1. Discuss some of the major themes and concepts you have learned from this Program.

2. How has your thinking been changed positively or negatively as a result of what you have learned in this Program?

3. How many different primates are there on Earth?

4. Why are traits such as skin color and hair texture insignificant in the study of primates?

5. Why is it important that the common person understand the new genetic findings scientist have discovered?

V. SUGGESTED ADDITIONAL BACKGROUND MATERIALS
Books:
Ashley, Maurice (2005). *Chess for Success: Using an Old Game to Build New Strengths in Children and Teens.* Broadway Books.

Freire, Paulo (1997). *Pedagogy of the Heart.* New York: The Continuum Publishing Company.

Internet Websites:
The Field Museum of Chicago   www.fieldmuseum.org

National Geographic Genographic Project   www.nationalgeographic.com/genographic

VI. KEY VOCABULARY
Evolution
Primates

DWD Anthology Glossary

AARP

The American Association of Retired Persons is an organization dedicated to increasing the quality of life of people 50 years of age and older.

Acculturation

The process of acquiring a second culture which is different from the one originally enculturated in.

Acquaintance

A person whom one knows only in one context like school.

African National Conference (ANC)

The ANC is the oldest national political party in the history of South Africa. The ANC helped lead the fight to end Apartheid and eventually led to the democratic election of Nelson Mandela.

Aged

The last stage in the human life cycle.

Alzheimer's Disease

A relative newly diagnosed degenerative brain disorder that develops in mid- to late adulthood. The common results are progressive and irreversible decline in memory and a deterioration of various other cognitive abilities. The disease is characterized by the destruction of nerve cells and neural connections in the cerebral cortex of ones brain and by a significant loss of brain mass which results in the loss of appropriate social behavior leading to hospitalization and or institutionalization.

Amish

A Christian group in North America, primarily composed of the Old Order of the Mennonite Church. The church originated in the late 17th century among followers of Jakob Ammann. The Amish are characterized by their lifestyle which minimizes the use of modern technology.

Amalgamation

The process by which a dominant group and a subordinate combine through intermarriage to form a new group.

American's with Disability Act (ADA)

Public Law 101-336, 104 Stat: 327 was signed into law on July 26, 1990 by President George H.W. Bush. It forbids discrimination based on disability.

Apartheid

South African term that in Afrikaans, literally means apartness. Generally refers to all forms of racial segregation. This was the governmental policy in South Africa from the early 1940's to the election of Mandela in 1994.

Androgyne/Androgynous/Androgyny

From the Latin roots for male (andro) and female (gyne). An androgynous person may identify and appear as both male and female, or as neither male nor female, or as in between male and female. This person also may or may not exhibit the behaviors of the two traditional genders, thus making it difficult for others to place them into a specific gender category.

Assimilation

The process by which an individual forsakes his or her own cultural tradition to become part of a different culture.

Association

A relationship resulting from participation in some formal or informal organization like a Program.

Bantustans

Referring to the self-governing South African states for Bantu (Native) people during Apartheid.

Best Friend

A confidant with whom one can share very personal information, a critic/advisor whose counsel is acceptable, a standard against which to measure oneself.

Bigot

A person who is intolerant to ideas and or positions different than their own.

Birds of paradise

A term referring to Italian men who lived in the United States but maintained relations in Italy by travelling back and forth between the two countries.

Bi-sexual

See Androgyne/Androgynous/Androgyny

Bombingham

A term coined during the Civil Rights movement referencing the number of bombings committed by Ku Klux Klan on the African American community in Birmingham, AL.

Coloureds

A South African term for people of mixed ancestry who largely live in the Cape area. This group also included East Indians and other Asians who were considered non-whites but enjoyed more privileges than the Native or dark skinned Africans of the region.

Context

The setting and environment in which a communication event takes place between two or more participants.

Creole

A term that has had many different meanings overtime, primarily used to refer to people of African and European descent who were born in the Americas. Originally from the Portuguese word crioulo, meaning a slave from Western Africa born in the New World.

Cues/Clues

Context information like the props in a CS that assist the actor in presenting the appropriate range of behaviors for a given event.

Cultural identity

The personal traits and values learned as part of an individual's membership in various microcultures such as ethnic or national origin, religion, gender, age, Program, language, geographic region, and exceptionality.

Cultural Scene (CS)

The information shared by two or more people that defines some aspect of their experience. CS is closely linked to recurrent social situations. Complex social organizations, like schools, provide numerous settings that qualify as CS.

Culture

The cognitive rules for appropriate behavior (including linguistic behavior) which are learned by people as a result of being members of the same group or community and also the perceptions, skills, knowledge, values, assumptions, and beliefs which underlie overt behaviors and are themselves shared products of group memberships.

Culture shock

Emotional stress produced by an absence of familiar signs and symbols in social intercourse, usually caused by exposure to a new culture.

Demography

The statistical study of human populations with special reference to size, density, distribution, and vital statistics.

Desensitization

The lack of compassion for human beings resulting from the over exposure to violence, suffering, and sexuality.

Dialect

Variations in a language as the result of geographic location.

Diaspora

Any scattering of dispersion of people with a common origin, background, or beliefs.

DNA

The molecular basis for heredity in many organisms.

Enculturation
   The development through the influence of parents with reinforcement by others in society of patterns of behavior in children that conform to the standards deemed appropriate by the culture (also called socialization).

Ethnicity
   The cultural and or linguistic differences of groups within a diverse society.

Ethnic group
   A microcultural group or collectivity that shares a common history and culture, common values, behaviors, and other characteristics that cause members of the group to have a shared identity.

Ethnocentrism
   A tendency to view alien cultures with disfavor and a resulting sense of inherent superiority.

Event
   A specific type of CS that involves people in purposeful activities acting on objects and interacting with each other to achieve some result.

Event Familiarity
   The amount of general knowledge an individual brings to a specific CS based on his/her propriospect which is necessary for accurate prediction of the event scenario and appropriate behavior.

Evolution
   Biological theory that animals and plants have their origin in other preexisting types and that the distinguishable differences are due to modifications in successive generations.

Feminism
   The rallying term for the political activism of Western Women in the 1960's and their development of a Female philosophy that impacts almost every aspect of patriarchal societies.

Fictive kinship
   The kinship-like relationship between persons not related by blood or marriage in a society, but who have become reciprocal social or economic relations.

French Quarter
   A notable tourist centre, its attractions include Mardi Gras and the French Quarter, a popular tourist area noted for its nightclubs and Creole architecture. It is also a medical, industrial, and educational centre.

Gay
   The quality or state of intense emotional and usually erotic attraction of a man to another man.

Glass ceiling
   The invisible forces that exist with in the economic structures of our society that limit the access of women and certain specific minority groups from obtaining senior leadership positions in the corporate world.

Global village
   The concept of referring to the earth's inhabitants as sharing a single interdependent community.

Handicapped
   An outdated term for people with disabilities.

Hegemony
   The dominant cultures means of enforcing conformity through the manipulation of media, education, and ideas that suggest the rightness of their position within society.

Heterosexist
   A person who is prejudice against people who are not a heterosexual.

High context cultures
   Societies in which the information within communication is contained in the physical context or is internalized within the people who are communicating.

Hip Hop

A cultural movement developed in New York City in the 1970's by African American and Latinos. Hip Hop is now a global phenomenon impacting youth culture all over the world. The major components of Hip Hop is DJing, emceeing, breakdance, and graffiti.

Homophobia

The fear of and prejudice toward homosexuality.

Hyper-masculinity

The overt testosterone driven behavior of males that can lead to the inappropriate treatment of females in a society.

Hyper-segregation

The over concentration of a ethnic group in a specific geographic area that often creates white flight.

Hypo descent

See Plessy v. Ferguson.

Idiolect

An individual's unique system of articulation. No two speakers operate a language in the "same" manner.

Indigenous

Native-born people of a region, or something produced or grown in a region.

Intersex

At least one in 2,000 children are born with some degree of ambiguity regarding their primary and/or secondary sex characteristics.

Islam phobia

The unreasonable fear of Islam and Muslim culture.

Islam

One of the major world religions founded by Muhammad in Arabia in the early 7th century AD. Believers total more than a billion and half people worldwide. The Arabic word Islam means "submission"-specifically, submission to the will of the one God, called Allah in Arabic. Islam is a strictly monotheistic religion, and its adherents, called Muslims, regard the Prophet Muhammad as the last and most perfect of God's messengers, who include Adam, Abraham, Moses, Jesus, and others. The sacred scripture of Islam is the Quran, which contains God's revelations to Muhammad. The religion is highly concentrated in Northern Africa, the Middle East and Asia.

Jazz

Musical form, often improvisational, developed by African Americans and influenced by both European harmonic structure and African rhythms.

Jim Crow

An enslaver whose name is associated solely with laws that whites passed legislating segregation and discrimination from the late 1800's to the late 1900's.

Jingoism

Extreme chauvinism or nationalism that often leads to excessive foreign policy.

Lesbian

The quality or state of intense emotional and usually erotic attraction of a woman to another woman.

Little Italy

The ethnic enclave for people of Italian heritage which is usually located in a large metropolitan area.

Low context cultures

Societies in which the communication is explicit and the message contains almost all of the information to be shared.

Macro-culture

The predominant core culture of a society. Even though the US has been influenced by a number of microcultures, it is probably most characterized by its WASP traits.

Micro-culture

One of many sub-cultures within a dominant multicultural society.

Muslim

See Islam.

MENSA

Mensa is an international society whose only qualification for membership is a score in the top 2 percent of the general population on a standardized intelligence test.

MC

A show business term meaning Master of Ceremonies (MC) that has been co-opted by the Hip Hop generation that refers to the Disc Jockey or person playing the music or rapping.

Mennonites

See Amish.

Misogyny

The male hatred of women.

Negative Recognition

The avoidance and rejection of individuals based on their physical characteristics, dress, language, and SES.

Novice

Within the context of Event Familiarity, a beginner or neophyte lacking the specific knowledge necessary for predicting the behaviors of others and the selection of their own appropriate behaviors for the given CS.

One drop rule

See Plessy v. Ferguson.

Opera Singers

A term used in reference to Italian men during WWII and one of the reasons Italians were not kept in detainment camps like the Japanese.

Paradigm

A conceptual model that serves as a cognitive map to organize experiences so that it has meaning and is comprehensible to the average observer. Basic paradigms provide the core assumptions about the nature of reality and set the boundaries for intellectual discourse.

Patriarchy

Societies that are dominated by males.

Persona

An individual's primary identity.

PFLAG

Parents Family and Friends of Lesbians and Gays

Plessey v Ferguson

The Supreme Court decision that said if a person's system has even one drop of African blood, that person is African and will be treated like other Africans; this decision established the separate-but-equal doctrine, which meant that African Americans and whites could have separate public facilities as they were equal.

Postmodernism

A basis for reexamining the basic structures, theories, and institutions of the modern world.

Prejudice

Unfavorable opinion or feeling formed beforehand without knowledge, thought, or reason.

Primates

One of more than 300 species of monkeys, apes, and other mammals of the order primate.

Propaganda
The manipulation of information to influence public opinion.

Propriospect
The sum total of an individual's experiences that enables him/her to make himself/herself intelligible to others well enough at least to permit him/her to accomplish many of his/her purposes through them.

Proxemics
The study of personal and cultural spatial needs and their interaction with their environmental space.

Powwows
Native American gatherings of dancing, singing, music playing, and visiting, accompanied by competitions.

Queer
A controversial term that some LGBT people still consider derogatory; others most often academics, political progressives and young people, have embraced the term because of its gender-neutrality and implication of social non-conformity.

Race
An invalid paradigm, developed to justify the different treatments accorded to different people.
A variety of Programification systems based on physical, linguistic and geographic characteristics.

Racialist
A belief in the goodness and rightness of ones race above all others.

Racism
Hatred that is based on the belief that race is the primary decider of a person's traits and capacities and that racial differences produce the inborn superiority of a particular race.

Recipes
Cognitive routines established over time through repetition to meet the needs of a particular situation. A way of economizing familiar episodes into a generalized episode.

Recognition
The acknowledgement or acceptance of another individual in any given CS.

Red lining
The pattern of discrimination against people trying to buy homes in minority and racially changing neighborhoods.

Resilience
The strength to endure and survive any kind of human hardship.

Red Apple
A pejorative term describing Native Americans who are red on the outside but white on the inside. A form of Uncle Tomism.

Rumspringa
An Amish practice that allows adolescence to experience mainstream cultures outside their community.

Saving face
Often associated with Asian cultures this a term that means not being disrespectful to others in public or taking actions so a person does not lose face in front of others.

Schema
Cultural schema are then abstract concepts people hold about the social world, including ideas about persons, roles, and events.

Scripts
Information that has already been established for anticipating what is to be expected and how the individual should act based on the constraints and cues present in any given situation.

Script Shifting
   The employment of a secondary script in a given context that may or may not be appropriate for the accomplishment of the primary script's intended goal.

Segregation
   The separation or isolation of a race, Program, or ethnic group by enforced or voluntary residence in a restricted area by barriers to social intercourse, by separate educational facilities, or by other discriminatory means.

Sexual Orientation
   The structure of our romantic, sexual, and/or emotional attractions. Some of the better-known categories include "heterosexual" (or "straight"), "homosexual" (or "gay" or "lesbian"), or "bisexual."

Shiites
   The second largest branch of Islam, Shiites currently account for 10%-15% of all Muslims. Shiite Islam originated as a political movement supporting Ali (cousin and son-in-law of Muhammad, the Prophet of Islam) as the rightful leader of the Islamic state.

Social Interaction Model (SIM)
   An analytical tool for observing and understanding human behavior in social contexts.

Skin Heads
   Member of an international youth subculture characterized by hair and dress styles evoking aggression and physical toughness.

Social Distance
   The patterns of acceptance and rejection toward cultural/ethnic groups held by individuals and manifested in their social interaction decisions in a society.

Social Persona
   The sum total of one's selected identities.

Socio Economic Status (SES)
   An index that describes such features as income, educational level, occupation, residency, and the organizations they belong to.

Sovereignty
In political theory, the ultimate authority in the decision-making process of the state and in the maintenance of order.

Social construction
   The process by which we construct reality by attributing meaning to the social experiences and behaviors of people in a society.

Status
   The combination of rights and duties in which individuals have social identities that are either ascribed or achieved.

Status Mobility System (SMS)
   The socially or culturally approved strategy for getting ahead within a given population or society. It is the people's folk theory of making it or getting ahead; however, the particular population defines getting ahead. (Ogbu, 1986)

Stereotypes
   A belief about other groups or individuals based on previously formed opinions and attitudes.

Sunnis
   The largest denomination of Muslims are the Sunni. They represent over 80% of all Muslims.

TAB
   The Temporarily Able-Bodied. A term that references the fact that all able-bodied humans run the risk of becoming disabled at some time during their life.

The Pillars of Islam
   The five duties incumbent of every Muslim are: the profession of faith in the one God and in Muhammad as his Prophet, praying five times a day, the giving of alms to the poor, fasting during the month of Ramadan, and the hajj or pilgrimage to Mecca.

Townships
See Bantustans.

Transgendered
Originally coined to describe non-operative transsexuals, this term now refers to people who do not identify with the gender roles assigned to them by society based on their biological sex. Transgender is also used as an umbrella term for all those who choose not to conform to society's often stereotypical notions of gender expression, including transsexuals, cross-dressers, two-spirit people, and drag queens and kings.

Understanding
The individual's ability to interpret the CS and activate the appropriate script/recipes to respond within the range of socially acceptable behavior.

Wave theory
A migration theory that suggests that in certain migration patterns the first group to relocate is composed of high level officials in government and the military, the well educated, and the urban elite; the second wave is composed of low-level officials, less educated merchants, and those seeking to be reunited with their families who have already left; the third wave brings the rural poor, the farmers, and the least educated.

White flight
The social phenomenon that describes the voluntary movement of European Americans from their neighborhoods and communities as a result of too many minorities moving in to their geographic area.

Xenophobia
The fear or hatred of strangers or foreigners.

Yellow journalism
The use of lurid features and sensationalized news in newspaper publishing to attract readers and increase circulation. The phrase was coined in the 1890s to describe the tactics employed in furious competition between two New York City newspapers, the World and the Journal

Zydeco
Zydeco is a popular accordion-based musical genre hailing from the prairies of south-central and southwest Louisiana. Contrary to popular belief, it is not Cajun in origin; rather, zydeco is the music of south Louisiana's Creoles of Color, who borrowed many of zydeco's defining elements from Cajun music

References for the Glossary:

Asante, M. K. (1995). *African American History: A Journey of Liberation.* The Peoples Publishing Group. Maywood, New Jersey.

Encyclopedia Britannica 2006 CD.

Grant, C.A. and Ladson-Billings, G. (1997). *Dictionary of Multicultural Education.* Oryx Press. Phoenix, AZ.

Samovar, L.A. and Samovar, R. E. (1991). *Communication Between Cultures.* Wadsworth Publishing Company, Belmont, California.

Saunders, C. and Southey, N. (1998). *A Dictionary of South African History.* David Philip Publishers, Cape Town, South Africa.

Schaefer, R.T. (2000). *Racial and Ethnic Groups, 8th Edition.* Prentice Hall, Upper Saddle River, New Jersey

Siragusa, N. (2001). *The Languge of Gender.* GLSEN.
www.glsen.org/cgi-bin/iowa/all/library/record/1646.html

Production Credits

Producer/Instructional Design
Yevette Lewis Brown

Director
Tony Labriola

Production/Research Assistant
Keisha Dyson

Video
Heather Penn
Tom Sauch

Audio
Archie Cocke

Floor Director
Susan Byars

Cameras
LeRon Bartlett.
Charles Klaas
Jeff Krohn
Mark Kundla

Editors
Mark Kundla
Tony Labriola

Editing Assistants
Karin Carlson
Jeff Krohn

Set /Lighting Design
Tony Labriola

Open Design
Archie Cocke

Set Art Work
Sergio Gomez

Graphics
Ann Needham
Christopher Sargent

Field Directors
Tony Labriola
Jon Tullos

Field Producers
David Ainsworth
Yevette Lewis Brown

Field Cameras
Nick Capodice
Cheri Dangoy-Niemiec
Mark Kundla

Field Audio
Mark Burda
Archie Cocke
Jack Mulder

Content Specialist
John Q. Adams, Ph.D.

Special Thanks:

National Geographic Genographic Project
A research partnership with IBM
www.nationalgeographic.com/genographic

"Crash" provided courtesy of Lionsgate Films

"Hip Hop: Beyond Beats and Rhymes" provided courtesy of God Bless the Child Productions

"Reel Bad Arabs" provided courtesy of Jack Shaheen and Media Education Foundation

"And They Came To Chicago: The Italian American Legacy"
provided courtesy of Gia Marie Amella, Modio Media and Italic Institute of America

"Hate.com: Extremists on the Internet" provided courtesy of HBO Films

A Production of the Division of Digital Learning and Media Design
Charles Nolley, Director
Governors State University
John Stoll, Dean

c. 2008 Governors State University

CPSIA information can be obtained
at www.ICGtesting.com
Printed in the USA
LVOW02s0500210516

488763LV00006B/11/P